101
Uses
for a
Dog

101 Uses for a Dog
Edited by Andrea Donner

© 2001 Willow Creek Press

Published by Willow Creek Press
P.O. Box 147 • Minocqua, Wisconsin 54548

Design: Pat Linder

For information on other Willow Creek titles,
call 1-800-850-9453

Library of Congress Cataloging-in-Publication Data

101 uses for a dog / edited by Andrea K. Donner.
        p. cm.
  ISBN 1-57223-500-4 (hardcover : alk. paper)
  1. Dogs--pictorial works. 2. Photography of dogs. I. Title: One hundred one uses for a dog. II. Title: One hundred and one uses for a dog. III. Donner, Andrea K.
  SF430 .A15 2001
  636.7'0022'2--dc21

                                    2001003688

Printed in Canada

101
Uses
for a
Dog

Willow Creek Press
Minocqua, Wisconsin

. . . in and
around
the house

2

Coffee table

3 *Groundskeeper*

5 *Alarm clock*

© Denver Bryan

© Spartasphoto.com

© Bonnie Nance

Bookmark

© Robert C. Hayes

© Sharon Eide / Elizabeth Flynn

© Bonnie Nance

© Denver Bryan

© Sharon Eide / Elizabeth Flynn

© Bonnie Nance

24

Someone who can't wait for you to come home.

. . . as
playmates

© Cheryl Ertelt

© William Meyer

© Ron Kimball Studios

© Bonnie Nance

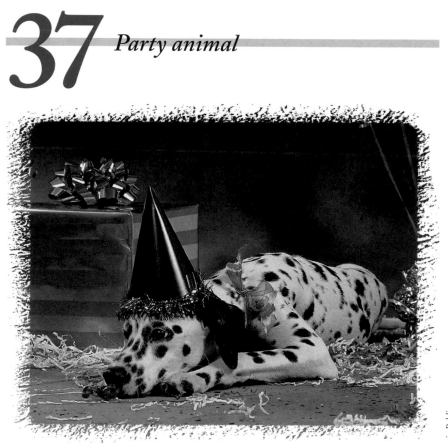

© Norvia Behling

© Cheryl Ertelt

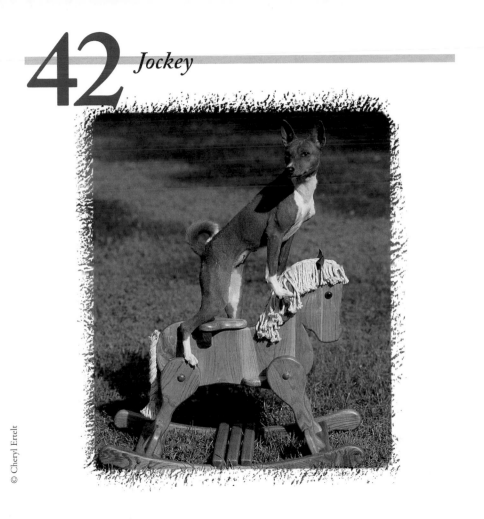

© Tara Darling

. . . as
tireless
helpers

© Cheryl Ertelt

© Bonnie Nance

69 *Paper boy*

. . . and
specialty
uses

75 *Peace keeper*

© Bonnie Nance

© Tara Darling

© Bonnie Nance

© Ron Kimball Studios

© Cheryl Ertelt

92 *...and to grow old with*

© Louisa Preston